SIMPLE
TRUTHS

Other Liguori/Triumph Titles
by Fulton J. Sheen

From the Angel's Blackboard
Jesus, Son of Mary
Lift Up Your Heart
Peace of Soul
Characters of the Passion
The Cross and the Beatitudes
Seven Words of Jesus and Mary

SIMPLE TRUTHS

Thinking Life Through with Fulton J. Sheen

LIGUORI/TRIUMPH
Liguori, Missouri

Published by Liguori/Triumph
An imprint of Liguori Publications
Liguori, Missouri
www.liguori.org

Library of Congress Cataloging-in-Publication Data

Sheen, Fulton J. (Fulton John), 1895–1979.
    Simple truths : thinking life through / with Fulton J. Sheen.
— 1st ed.
        p.   cm.
    ISBN 978-0-7648-0169-3
    1. Christian life—Catholic authors. 2. Christian life—
Quotations, maxims, etc.   I. Title.
BX2350.2.S457 1998
248.4'82—dc21   97–24513

Compilation Copyright © 1998 by the Estate of Fulton J. Sheen
Printed in the United States of America
16 15 14 13 12 / 14 13 12 11 10

SIMPLE
TRUTHS

"Do we find existence, truth, and love in their plenitude on this earth? Do we carry within ourselves the potencies to realize them in the higher degree? We possess a modicum of life, a modicum of truth, and a modicum of love, but do we possess them in their entirety?"

—*Fulton J. Sheen*

"There is a quest that calls me
In nights when I am alone,
The need to ride where the ways divide
The Known from the Unknown.
I mount what thought is near me
And soon I reach the place,
The tenuous rim where the Seen grows dim,
And the sightless hides its face.
I have ridden the wind,
I have ridden the sea,
I have ridden the moon and stars,
I have set my feet in the stirrup seat
Of a comet coursing Mars.
And everywhere
Thro' the earth and ear
My thought speeds, lightning-shod,
It comes to a place where checking pace
It cries, 'Beyond lies God.' "

—*Cale Young Rice*

CONTENTS

FOREWORD

Dost thou love life?
Then do not squander time,
for that's the stuff life is made of.
—Benjamin Franklin

When we think about our life, we often think in terms of time: the first time…, the time when…, the happy times, the sad times. We think, too, of eternity: the time to come. We realize that life is a continuum, and that this earthly life is but a fleeting moment in Time, a passageway to Life. The words of Benjamin Franklin, therefore, echo true when we pause to reflect on life's meaning—who we are, why we are, where we are, where we are going, and how we might get there.

Such reflection is bound to yield the greatest truth of all: We are made for God; we are made to share eternity with Him. And it was that singular truth to which Fulton J. Sheen dedicated his ministry in all its forms. His was a crusade to bring souls to God, to win Heaven for all humanity, and, as was often remarked, "to reconcile the world to Christ." Hence, his spoken and written words were offered to assist all who struggle through life, particularly when priorities are not clear—or just plain out of line.

It is difficult in this fast-paced world, amid the clamors for our attention, to find time to step back, to see things more clearly, to evaluate our life and reassess our priorities. This small book is meant to help us do just that. Grouped under the categories of Faith, Hope, Love, and Truth, these short passages of simple wisdom speak truths that we often lose sight of, the simple truths that sustain us through life, if we but take time to ponder: truths about God's limitless power; virtue and goodness; grace and forgiveness; faith and freedom; love and loss; self and others; silence and activity; time and eternity.

Drawn primarily from Sheen's newspaper columns, as well as a few lately (re)discovered other sources, this collection of Simple Truths has been a joy to compile. The resurgent popularity of Sheen's writings attests to his giftedness in tapping the pulse of a culture and bringing Light where before there was darkness. And so, it came as no surprise to find in these sources such a treasury of practical wisdom and directions for right Christian living that I wanted to share them with readers everywhere.

May these pages, filled with timeless Light, bring a sense of balance and purpose to all who read them. And most of all, may we hold firm on the one and only course set before us, walking the walk from the City of Man to the City of God.

PATRICIA A. KOSSMANN
LITERARY REPRESENTATIVE
THE ESTATE OF FULTON J. SHEEN

Part One

⟨◇⟩

LIVING IN FAITH

"Faith is the substance
of things hoped for,
the evidence
of things not seen."
—*Hebrews 11:1*

*I*f anyone will look closely into the experiences of life, he will discover that God is in some way giving us a more inward sense of things, as if He would not let us become lodged in the temporal, but shove us on to what is beyond.

The eternal is with us more than we know, and even when we refuse to face it.

*T*o those who act on what they know, more shall be revealed. Christ said: "If you do My will, you will have My Doctrine." Increase of faith will come from virtue more than from study.

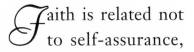

*F*aith is related not to self-assurance, but to God; not to an event, but to truth. In fact, there is often the greatest faith when there is the least prosperity. Such was the case with Job who, full of sores and sitting on a dung hill, said: "I will trust Him though He slay me."

*F*aith begins at a point where there is seemingly nothing to get out of it; nor is there any indication that prosperity will follow. Faith begins with a considerable doubt about one's own goodness and power.

*T*here are two ways of knowing how good God is: One is never to lose Him; the other is to lose Him and find Him again!

*T*ry meditation for at least fifteen minutes a day, and in the end you will make two great discoveries: what you really are, and what you are on the way to becoming.

No believer ever went into the Gethsemane of bitter grief, but that he found his Master had gone "a little farther."

Religion is not a sum of beliefs that we would like, but the sum of beliefs God has given.

How different is the soul that has built for itself a sanctuary within, where his strength is God, regardless of what may happen on the outside.

*I*t is reason that creates motives for believing. Faith is to religion very much like credit is to business. Just as one must have a reason for giving credit, so, too, one must have a reason for believing. The conclusions of reason for accepting the testimony of anyone—for example, the testimony of Christ—are not mathematically certain. They are only morally certain. They are very much like the certitude that you have that you were born of your own parents.

There are some things we outgrow in adulthood, but one of them is not virtue. This world is only a nursery, or better, the cradle in which souls, yet in swaddling bands, are rocked into immortality.

As one carries the physical equipment of birth through life, so one carries the spiritual equipment one receives on the other side of eight. What is fed on the spoon to the child is what he will eat from the table as a man.

$\mathcal{A}$fter your car is filled with gasoline, it will not drive itself.

Grace will move you only when you want it to move you, and only when you let it move you.

$\mathcal{W}$e are living in a day of grace and of faith. God's seeming apathy in the presence of suffering of His people is part of the discipline of the life of faith. And yet there is something seen in the hearts of those who suffer. They pass from a world that is not worthy of them to the Home that God has prepared for them: "They endured at seeing Him Who is invisible."

Very often the greater the dependence on God, the more power there is over the things of the earth. Saint Francis had a power over birds and animals which is not given to many mortals. Other saintly souls have had the power of working miracles.

The more one is an instrument in the hand of God, the more readily God works through that instrument. If a pencil rebelled against the direction of the hand, less writing would be done. The more supple the instrument, the greater the communication of power.

Ask a patient with a broken bone: "Does it hurt you?" And he, very likely, will answer: "Not when I keep it still." Peace of soul is found in that calm, when once a week we open windows to heaven.

Most of us are in prison walls; we would like to do other work than that which is forced upon us. Shall we break under it, complain and rebel, or shall we use the time to the profit of our souls?

*G*andhi was once asked: "If you were given the power to remake the world, what would you do first?" He answered, "I would pray for the power to renounce that power." God's method in dealing with us is self-surrender. Give up what is less to achieve the greater.

*A*s a bird in an egg can never fly, so we can never become a new creature unless we crack the shells and are helped in our hatching by Him Who says: "I would gather thee to myself as the hen gathers her chicks."

*T*he many miracles of Our Blessed Lord opening the eyes of the blind were symbols of His opening the unbelief of hearts to the truth of His revelation. Saint Paul himself was spiritually blind, and tells the story of how his eyes were opened spiritually on the road to Damascus. At the very moment that he received the full impact of the meaning of human life, Christ spoke to him saying: "Thou shalt open their eyes and turn them from darkness to light, from the power of Satan to God, so that they may receive through faith in Me, the remission of their sins and inheritance among the saints."

Our knowledge of Truth will be cumulative, if we really wish it to grow:

"Ask and the gift will come; seek and you shall find; knock and the door shall be opened to you."

One of the interesting psychological effects of traveling is to go to a spot where one hears no news for a week. How calm the heart becomes! It is not because one does not know what is going on in the world, but rather because one does not know so many bad things that are going on in the world.

Listening to woes makes one like the man who dropped a bottle that broke into pieces and then gathered all of the broken glass and put it to his bosom, where it cut him constantly.

When the heart is filled with the supreme and transcendent desire after the Eternal God, then one realizes that there are no accidents in life—everything comes from His Hands. Dust never rises very high on the road; the birds which fly high above have no dust upon their wings. So the heart that knows how to fly high enough escapes the anxieties and the worries which brood upon the earth.

If everything in the world were perfectly good we would still need God, for goodness comes from God.

Why should a confessor stand between my God and me? For the same reason that the human nature of Christ stands between His divinity and me.

A martyr must die for the faith, not for his property, nor his good name, nor for the sake of the party. Self-made martyrs are numerous, but they have no place in the ranks of those who are promised the Kingdom of Heaven for taking the Cross of Christ on their shoulders.

The measure of the faith we have in the Inner Presence of Divinity in the soul is the measure of our light in darkness and strength in moments of trial. Those who have been to the top of the Alps witness that they have seen rain fall under them, but not one drop ever falls on them.

Those who have God as their protection have an inner tower that is never depressed by adversity nor inflated by pride in moments of success and prosperity.

*I*n the prayer of communion, the ear is more important than the tongue. We learned the language we speak through listening; so, too, knowledge comes from listening. He who does all the talking in prayer is not praying. Scripture says: "Speak, Lord, for Thy servant heareth"—not "Listen, Lord, for thy servant speaketh." There eventually comes an experience when, through contact with Divine Power, one hardly ever expresses any wish except to do the Will of God. God never is a means to the self-realization of our egotistic ambitions; rather, we become the means of glorifying and loving Him.

The astronomer does not give up his science because he does not find a new planet every day; the poet does not give up poetry because he cannot write brilliant verses every day. But the ideal of science and the ideal of poetry remain. So virtue, faith, and the abiding resolve to save one's soul remain even when one does not "feel" like saving one's soul. Ideals must never be left to the mercy of the stomach or the glands. They reside in the will. Hence the Divine Truth reminded us: "He who perseveres unto the end will be saved."

The Divine order to worship one day a week is for the sake of meditation for the mind; the seasons with their light and heat, their spring and winter, all suggest some escape from the material and the economic. The hand is not most properly seen when it is pressed against the eye, nor do our problems appear in their proper perspective except when viewed from afar. Even the spiritual faculties are subject to the same law as Our Blessed Lord told His apostles: "Come away into a quiet place by yourselves and rest a little."

$\mathcal{S}$ix days are as-
signed to work by
the Divine Command, but one day a
week we are to break with the commer-
cial and the material, by turning from
the physical to the spiritual. Stopping
work is not breaking the current with
the pursuit of profit or pleasure.

Worship is contact, or the unplugging
of ourselves from the muddled darkness of the plow, in order to allow God
to flow into our hearts.

*P*atience is not a Stoic apathy or a senseless gritting of the teeth in a vain display of what one can endure; it is no narcotic virtue to stupefy and take away the sense of affliction. Basically, it is a quiet, calming, and willing submission to the Hand of God.

*T*o be pure in heart is to make purity everywhere. The pure of heart shall see God in nature's mirror and in science, in creation's visions and the voices of every color. They will see Him in His Providence. They will even see Him in the mysteries they cannot understand.

To have the courage to look into ourselves is the beginning of a dialogue that takes place between the mask and the face, the shadow self and the real self. Once this dialogue has been achieved honestly, then there opens another dialogue: that of the soul with God.

We cannot have communications with heaven until we have communications with ourselves.

$\mathcal{D}$emosthenes became the great orator because he had a weakness of speech. Would we ever have had the poems of Elizabeth Barrett Browning if her spirit had not overcome the sufferings when her spine was injured by a fall from a horse, when she was kept a prisoner in her father's house until she married, and when as an invalid, she spent most of her life propped up on a couch by cushions? The sparks of her love poetry came not from one who bemoaned her pain, but from one who saw in it all the "shade of God's Hand outstretched caressingly."

Circumstances, whatever they be, are occasions for the acceptance and working of Divine Power.

*T*he less we are certain of the purpose of living, the more we hurry to "kill" time. Whoever loses his way will always drive faster.

Holy people never hurry; their vision of timelessness gives them time. "They who have faith do not hurry," the Old Testament prophet tells us.

*T*o have any effectiveness, a prayer for help must express an honest desire to be changed, and that desire must be without reservation or conditions on our part.

*C*heer may be natural, in which case it springs from an inborn vitality and zest for living. Even those who lack it can cultivate it to some extent, as marching music lessens fatigue.

But there is another kind of cheerfulness which is Divine in origin. Saint Paul bade others to have it as believing in God. This counsel he spoke to others in the midst of a storm at sea, promising them relief and rescue without loss of life. This kind of cheerfulness is found in Francis of Assisi, who expressed the joy of grace in his soul by song. Teresa of Ávila, who lived a life of great penance, was wont to pour out her joy in that inner world of spirituality by clapping her hands and dancing in the Spanish style.

In the history of the world there never has been a sad saint, because sanctity and sadness are opposites.

*I*t is not true to say that we would all be heroic if our trials were on a great scale. The Divine Master said that only he who was faithful in the little things would be put over the great things. Heroism in the least is the pledge of heroism in the greatest. Unless we can bear up under the trifling trials, we go down under the great ones.

$\mathcal{A}$ saint is one who puts forth the same amount of energy in developing justice, charity, joy, and peace as the very prosperous business executive puts forth in making money. It may even take less energy to be a saint than a millionaire, because the saint is assured of the help of God, while the millionaire is not because he has to rely on his own efforts.

Léon Bloy once wrote that the greatest tragedy in all the world is not being a saint. He did not put sanctity very far beyond the reach of anyone, when he added: "One step beyond mediocrity, and we are saints."

Outside and beyond all our scientific, political, and economic fads which make the news of the hour on the hour, there are other kinds of knowledge and other truths which are eternal. These are the great truths of faith, such as redemption from sin and oneness with the Divine Life—which alone are the source of true peace of soul. But even these truths we know only in part. We see the way the road is leading and we enjoy walking it; but we have not yet entered into the City.

If it be asked why God does not reveal more of His truth here, the answer is that He has revealed enough to give us certainty of committing our entire life to Him. Furthermore, our poor minds have not the absorptive power of much Infinite Truth; a purification of mind is required, which the saints but dimly achieve. It is presently enough to know that the purification of our lives is the condition of finding this expanded knowledge in eternity.

*O*ne can never really understand his vocation in life until he first becomes a person, and one never becomes a person until he is inner-driven, and one is never inner-driven until he dialogues with God. This is what meditation is all about.

*P*ermissiveness means the absence of restraints or discipline, allowing weeds to grow in the garden.

In contrast to permissiveness is the Divine injunction: "Enter by the narrow gate."

*T*he eclipse of the sun is really never in the sun itself, but in some object that obtrudes itself between the sun and the eye. The eclipse of faith is not in the source of faith, but in some deliberate frustration in the rays of grace. If the eye is evil, the whole body is in darkness. The cataract eye never sees things whole; the prejudiced eye sees truth distorted.

$\mathcal{F}$reedom that ignores the transcendent difference between good and evil ends in the denial of freedom itself.

$\mathcal{A}$mong the most astounding words of Christ are: "Whoever has the will to do the Will of God shall know whether My teaching comes from Him or is merely My own."

$\mathcal{A}$s soon as a religious person ceases to think about the next world, he becomes ineffective in this one. It is only when we aim at heaven that this world is thrown in. Those who

live by this principle are the coura-
geous. With John Donne, they say: "I
need Thy thunder, O God, Thy songs
no longer suffice us."

Contentment is the
virtue of being sat-
isfied with whatever state or condition
in which we find ourselves. It consists
not so much in adding fuel to the fire
as in taking some fire away; not in mul-
tiplying wealth, but in diminishing desires, in realizing that thirst can better be quenched out of a cup than out
of a river.

$\mathcal{A}$long with Silence, there must go a sense of the Presence of God. This means begging the Divine Light to illumine our hearts to see it not as we think we are, or as others think we are, but as we really are in the sight of God.

Dr. Paul Tournier, the distinguished Swiss psychiatrist, made meditation "my first and most urgent appointment. As a general rule, I do not see patients before nine o'clock," he said. "In this way, I have two-and-a-half hours available at the beginning of every day in which I can meditate, read the Bible or some other spiritual treasures of world literature, examine my faults of the day before, and prepare my day in God's presence."

*A*ll evils become lighter if we endure them patiently, but the greatest benefits can be poisoned by discontent. The miseries of life are sufficiently deep and extensive, without our adding to them unnecessarily.

*G*od walks into your soul with silent step. God comes to you more than you go to Him.

Never will His coming be what you expect, and yet never will it disappoint. The more you respond to His gentle pressure, the greater will be your freedom.

*I*f you have grown flowers, have you not sometimes put a pot over the growing plant, momentarily keeping it in temporary darkness that it might gain strength? How often sorrow has brought out some latent generosity or energized some unusual faculty of strength.

We are not yet what we can become.

Part Two

⊰◈⊱

LIVING IN HOPE

"Hope springs eternal
in the human breast;
Man never Is,
but always To be blest."
—*Alexander Pope*

*O*ur citizenship is in Heaven. We are here in an order to which we outwardly belong, but in the depths of our being we belong to another order altogether. The essential of Christian life, therefore, is to look forward to the city of Heaven, for here we have no continuing city, but live among the transient, temporal things. This was the meaning of the Jewish Feast of Tabernacles, a reminder that we are pilgrims and we live here to complete our existence.

As the strong must see their moral weakness, so the weak must see their moral strength. Each is of irreplaceable worth in the eyes of God and of greater value than any neighbor who despises him.

God has given different gifts to different people. There is no basis for feeling inferior to another who has a different gift. Once it is realized that we shall be judged by the gift we have received, rather than the gift we have not, one is completely delivered from a sense of false inferiority.

The end of an old year makes one hear the injunction God gave to Moses: "You will not tread that way again." Though time indeed cannot be turned back, the faults and failings of time are not fixed and unalterable. Divine Pardon can make them non-existent. Magdalenes can have fires that burned inward changed into fires that burn upward; Pauls who hate can learn to burn with zeal.

The essence of the Gospel is the blessing of the second chance.

*B*eauty on the outside never gets into the soul, but beauty of the soul reflects itself on the face. Its loveliness refuses to be imprisoned; it comes out in the eyes, the words, and the kindness of the hands. The luster of holiness, however much it reveals itself on the outside, has to be kept up by contact with its spiritual fountain.

As the sun in the sky shines on clouds and makes them beautiful, so the Divine Light can even make more beautiful the faces that are clouded with sorrows and freighted with tears.

$\mathcal{A}$ venerable old man a few centuries after Paul gave this secret of his contentment: "It consists in nothing more than in making the right use of my eyes. In whatever state I am, I first of all look up to heaven, remembering that my spiritual business here is to get there; then I look down upon the earth and recall how small a place I occupy in it when I die. From that moment on, I am content."

$\mathcal{W}$ hen we pick out the worst in people, we drive them to hatred or despair; when we tell them we expect better things, they are given hope.

It is one thing to be so mastered by conditions outside of us that they can make us sad and gloomy when they fail to satisfy us; it is quite another thing to be so master of what is outside that nothing that ever happens changes our spiritual condition. The reason we do not perish as the earth revolves about the sun is because the earth carries its own atmosphere.

So he who carries a sense of Providence amidst the trials of earth is never depressed.

The best way to enjoy old age is to see in it a time for making up for the sins that went before, and living in hope for the joys that lie ahead. But this takes faith!

What makes our moment in history arduous is our failure to see the relation between things, so bent have we been on their disruption and destruction. But God never really abandons a world, though the world abandons Him. He can take those very elements of nature which turned against Him, and make them the instruments of redemption.

*A*ge has many purposes that are good and holy. The Old Testament makes old age the reward for obedience to parents. Saint Paul speaks of age as a merciful gift of Providence to enable us to do penance for the sins of youth. Age also becomes the fountain of wisdom and experience from which the young may drink.

Michelangelo, who lived to be almost ninety, often used to repeat his motto as he chiseled marble that almost spoke: "I still learn." Cicero claimed that age gave stability to reason by the quieting of the passions. Almost all fruits grow sweeter as they approach the time of plucking.

Age is more merciful than youth. It was the young men who counseled David to be cruel; the old counseled him to be merciful. Those who have the faith, and live virtuously, dwell in radiant expectation of the glory that is to come.

$\mathcal{I}$n the area of religion, the secret of courage is: "I will fear no evil, for Thou art with me." Responsibilities are no longer burdensome if one realizes that the Divine works in us. Want of courage is want of faith.

There are no limits to the truth you can know, to the life you can live, to the love you can enjoy, and to the beauty you can experience.

When the masses attempted to make Our Lord a King, He fled into the mountain alone. Before He chose His disciples, He went into a mountain retreat and prayed. When the apostles came back with a report of the success of their activity, He bade them retire into a desert place for contemplation. Before He began His mission or His public life, He went into the wilderness.

It may, therefore, be that in the very heart of loneliness, there is opportunity for spiritual growth and mental refreshment and enlightened vision. Loneliness may not be the terrible thing it is believed to be. Achievement can start in loneliness. Solitude can be very rewarding and full of blessing because in the silence of the inner being, one finds God.

We do not need to fear the malice of hearts open to God's inspection, as all human hearts are. For if God is on our side, what does it matter who tries to act against us?

Why is it that the absurdities of life lead some minds to despair, while the same trials lead others to hope and inner peace? It is because in the second group the struggle is worth our best, knowing that God is not in heavenly headquarters calling the shots, but Himself coming down into the muck and mud of all this meaninglessness, overcoming the evil that caused it and giving us the strength to do the same.

We already have enough critics; now our poor world needs apostles of encouragement. But whence shall they come except from Hope born of a Loving and Merciful Savior?

Belief in the Resurrection of Christ does not start with the fact of the empty tomb, nor only with the fact that dead men rise. It begins with the truth that crucified men rise. In other words, only those who have in some way presided over the crucifixion of their pride and selfishness ever know what it is to rise from the dead. They become "new creatures."

*G*od could never let you suffer a pain or a reversal or experience sadness if it could not in some way minister to your perfection. If He did not spare His own Son on the Cross for the redemption of the world, then you may be sure that He will sometimes not spare your wants that you might be all you need to be: happy and perfect children of a loving Father.

He may even permit us to wage wars as a result of our selfishness that we may learn there is no peace except in Goodness and Truth.

"Be still and know that I am God." Activism does not make theologians. Many are not sure of God because they are never quiet. The failure of the churches today is due in part to their being so exteriorized. From time to time, they should ask for a hush to life to lose the voices of the world. The voice of God is heard only in quiet.

Good tidings are at everyone's door, if they would stop talking and listen to the knock.

$\mathcal{M}$an is at his worst if he falls into despair; but he is at his best if, humbled, he cries to God for help.

To solve our cares God must not only be Personal, He must also be in the dust of human cares. That is why He, with full understanding of our troubles, can say: "Come to Me, all ye who labor and are heavily burdened and find rest for your souls."

$\mathcal{C}$hrist achieved the re-creation of man through His own Person; it remains for us to apply it to ourselves and through ourselves to the material universe, so that all things might be restored in Him.

The essence of Christianity consists not in obeying a set of commands, nor in submitting to certain laws, nor in reading Scripture, nor in following the example of Christ. Before all else, it consists in being re-created, re-made, and incorporated into the Risen Christ, so that we live His life, think His thoughts, and will His love.

God can draw good out of evil because, while the power of doing evil is ours, the effects of our evil deeds are outside our control, and, therefore, in the hands of God.

*T*ears are not without value, provided one sees a purpose in their shedding. As the morning rose is sweetest when embalmed with dew, so "love is loveliest when embalmed in tears." Many a person sees God through tears more often than in the sunlight; in fact, tears may leave the vision of the eyes clear for stars.

*P*ain in itself is not unbearable; it is the failure to understand its meaning that is unbearable. If that thief [on the cross] did not see purpose in pain, he would never have saved his soul. Pain can be the death of our soul, or it can be its life.

The life of the body is the soul; the life of the soul is Christ. Because grace or supernatural life is a regeneration, it makes no difference what your background is, nor how wicked you may have been, nor how many sins you committed. Once you make God's life your own, by an act of will, you live by a new Spirit, are governed by new laws, breathe a different atmosphere, and have an entirely new set of values.

57

*N*ever believe those who say: "Once a thief, always a thief" or "you are wasting your money on that worthless creature." The Christian claim is: You are not!

You can put off your old nature and put on a new. Since grace is regeneration, it makes little difference what your old nature was. If I throw away an old coat, it makes little difference if I did so because it is torn, or because it is spotted with soup, or because it is moth-eaten, or because it is faded. The only thing that matters is: I throw it away. And when I throw it away, I get a new coat.

The difference is that by being reborn in Christ, you do not throw away something external; you bury your nature with Christ. You do it because you get a new nature, one that partakes of the very nature of God. In the strong language of Saint John: "We are born of God."

*W*ill eternity be anything like what I have seen, or what I have heard, or what I can imagine? No, eternity will be nothing like anything I have seen, heard, or imagined. "Eye has not seen, nor ear heard, neither has it entered into the heart of man, what things God has prepared for those who love him."

*J*ust as the past is not as antiquated as some would believe, so the future is not as futuristic as the planners have planned. The reason is that in making any kind of prediction, one must distinguish the future that depends on science and technology from the future that depends on human factors.

The truth is, the future is in our souls, and our communion with the God of Love; otherwise we shall just exist, and on our tombstone will be written: "Nothing ever happened to him."

When God takes someone from us, it is always for a good reason. When the sheep have grazed and thinned the grass in the lower regions, the shepherd will take a little lamb in his arms, carry it up the mountain where the grass is green, lay it down, and soon the other sheep will follow.

Every now and then Our Lord takes a lamb from the parched field of a family up to those Heavenly Green Pastures, that the rest of the family may keep their eyes on their true home and follow through.

No life is too far spent to be recouped; no lifelong idleness precludes a few minutes of useful work in the vineyard of the Lord, even the last few hours of life, as was the case with the penitent thief.

God loves you despite your unworthiness. It is His love which will make you better, rather than your betterment which will make Him love you. Often during the day say: "God loves me, and He is on my side, by my side."

*A*ll souls are precious, even though they should remain lost in a corner under dust for years.

There is a homecoming for everyone, because there is a Father and there is a heaven.

Part Three

LIVING IN LOVE

"Love conquers all things:
let us too give in to Love."
—*Virgil*

$\mathcal{I}$f people only know how happy they would make themselves if they really helped their neighbor for the love of God, we would soon become a nation with songs in our hearts, as well as on our lips.

$\mathcal{T}$here might be less spiritual blindness in the world if those who had the light obeyed the Divine injunction: "Let your light shine before all."

The person who is caught up in the whirlpool of life can never extricate another from its whirling waters. Martha, who was busy about many things, was not as good at advising others as Mary, who sat at the feet of the Master in quiet and contemplation.

As Thomas Aquinas so wisely put it: Contemplata aliis tradere—We deliver to others those things upon which we have meditated.

Why did the Lord find Himself in the company of publicans, sinners, harlots, and wine bibbers? It was certainly not because of the way they lived, nor to defend their causes. It was partly because they were not attempting to prove their own virtue, partly because society had already condemned them, and partly because they were already honest with themselves and wanted to be better. They wore no masks.

There is a world of difference between a gift and a sacrifice. A sacrifice is a gift plus the love and personality of the giver. A gift comes out of the pocketbook; a sacrifice out of the heart.

Constantly peering into ourselves to find our identity is very much like trying to catch ourselves going to sleep; we are asleep before we know we are asleep; we know things before we know that we know.

The way to self is from without; true identity seeks first oneness with those who need help.

$\mathcal{N}$othing so much destroys personality as the sense of self-importance. Its first demand is that everything should be as we wish, and as soon as it is not we complain to God and are annoyed by people.

The supreme height of spiritual loveliness is to be lovely and not know it.

$\mathcal{J}$oy never comes to those who seek it. In the self-forgetting hour when we are touched by another's need and sacrifice for it, we suddenly find our soul aflame with glorious joy.

$\mathcal{M}$an responds because he is called, as God calls because He needs. Like a magnet and steel, like the law of gravity and the fall of a star, there is a mutuality.

If one can imagine a hidden treasure in a field wishing to be found, one has the simple image of one capable of love wanting to be captured.

$\mathcal{M}$others in the animal kingdom care only for a body; mothers in the human kingdom must care also for a soul…a mind…a heart.

The tragedy of the world is that so many are unloved. Roses always look beautiful and smell sweet, and hence they are a prize to be possessed. Sweetbriar, however, has fragrant leaves, and they are never so fragrant as when it rains. The common people of the world are like these leaves; they have something fragrant about them, particularly when the days are dark and clouded and rain falls in their lives.

Anyone can love a rose; but it takes a great heart to love a leaf.

*G*entleness is never weakness, but power clothed in sympathy—as the Gentle Christ was the Omnipotence of God wrapped in swaddling bands.

*I*t is not enough merely to have an intellectual understanding of another's difficulty; we need to go a little farther to feel it as our own burden.

*N*o work is hard where there is love.

The spirit of community or togetherness is better achieved where there is the surrender of self for another. That is why Our Lord sent out His disciples two by two in order that they could practice charity one to another.

Any form of asceticism that disrupts charity is wrong. This was the mistake of the monk who decided to live only on crusts and upset the whole monastery, by making all the monks hunt for crusts to satisfy his desire for mortification.

Asceticism that makes us less agreeable to our neighbors does not please God.

*I*t is so important to listen to persons who come to us for help. They reveal not only themselves; they reveal ourselves to ourselves and make us say: "There go I but for the grace of God."

*O*nce I surrender the tinsel to have the jewel, then I enter into the mystery of love. I see that I do not love anyone unless he has some goodness in him, or is lovable in some way. But, I see also that God did not love me because I am lovable. I became lovable because God poured some of His Goodness and Love into me. I then begin to apply this charity to my neighbor. If I do not find him lovable, I have to put love into him as God puts love into me, and thereby I provoke the response of love. Now, my personality is restored and I make the great discovery that no one is happy until he loves both God and neighbor.

The people who are summoned to inherit the Kingdom are those who fed the hungry, clothed the naked, visited the sick. An open hand comes from a religious heart.

*L*ove is the inspira-tion of all sacri-fice. And love, be it understood, is not the desire to have, to own, to possess—that is selfishness. Love is the desire to be had, to be owned, to be possessed.

*L*ove is patient, tol-erant, benevolent. It extends to those beyond our own set and is exercised not only to the good, but even toward the dull and the foolish who stumble. But to be patient with them requires that kind of love which sees in every single person an immortal soul, more precious to the Lord than the universe itself.

There are some parents who use their authority by abusing the right to command, leaving to the child only the activity of submission, even in the smallest details. The first disobediences of children are generally born of this saturation with "don'ts." On the contrary, to respect the spontaneity of the child is to favor his obedience. It is one thing to say: "Go wash your hands, they are dirty." It is another thing to say: "What do you think of your hands?"

Liberty of thought always favors obedience.

Sometimes the greatest influences in the world are unconscious and indirect; they issue forth from dedication to God's truth, which is the primary concern. When one dwells in a royal bounty of Christlike goodness in himself, then his shadow falling on others makes them happy.

Voluntary influence does not always indicate what a person really is, but an involuntary influence always does.

Love dies when it becomes a fixation, for it is not a state but a process.

The ground of Divine rewards is in the service rendered, and not in the work itself. Thus they who produce great results will not be honored more than those people who produce less striking results. The poor, simple, uneducated people with one talent, who are equally faithful with smaller gifts, will receive the same reward.

It is not the ownership of talents that determines the judgment, but rather the enrichment of any talent that one possesses. Because one cannot do much, one is not excused from doing little.

Touch destroys anonymity, replacing it with personality. The peak of anonymity is reached in driving an automobile. Fortified by a ton or more of steel, one curses and blasts "Sunday drivers" or the one who cuts in front of one's car, giving a dirty look at X5Y382. If at the stoplight, one discovers that the person who cut us off is actually a friend, how the picture changes! But once we enter into communication, he or she ceases to be a functionary and immediately becomes personalized.

*W*hy *worship* God? Worship is a sign of value, the price we put on a service or a person. For example, when you applaud an actor on the stage or a returning hero, you are "worshiping" him in the sense of putting a value on his worth. When you take off your hat to a lady, you are "worshiping" her. To worship God means to acknowledge in some way His Power, His Goodness, and His Truth.

The soundest psychological advice ever given was: "If you wish to save your life, lose it." Forget for the moment self-importance; look to the values of others who do not belong to your set or class.

One can never love in a hurry.

Once love is put on a pedestal as an idol god, it is soon discovered that the stem of human affection cannot bear its weight. This is not to demean human love; it is only to insist that it is only human—a spark that falls from the great hearth of love, which is God.

The Holy Spirit of God is the source of your inspiration and guidance. In moments of crisis and doubt, in worries, listen to the voice of the Spirit within. The union of your soul and the Holy Spirit can become a kind of spiritual marriage, giving the joys of the spirit born of a unity that leaves all other joys as sorrows and all other beauty as pain. For the first time in your life, you will begin to love not that which is lovely, but that which is Love: the Spirit of the Most High God.

$\mathcal{R}$ecently, I heard a condemnation of the poor starving people of India: "Why did they not get out and make more, like I did?" The speaker made his money out of oil. He did not put it there; it just splashed up in his face. But the poor of India could dig until the end of time and not hit oil.

He who is constitutionally proud thinks himself a hundred times better than anyone else thinks of him.

$\mathcal{H}$ere is the secret of helping others: Treat them as we find them—not as they ought to be, not as we want them to be, but as they actually are. Later on, one can lift them up; but at the beginning there must be acceptance. This is always the way of the physician. The more accurately he can diagnose the actual state of the patient, the better prepared he will be to use his healing art. If, however, in the moral order, we throw books at the unfortunate one, we no more help them than a medical doctor will set a broken bone by reading a treatise to the patient on the dangerous effects of broken bones.

Self-expression is not a simple matter. It may mean the expression of self to the detriment of others, or the suppression of self for the sake of the expression of the rights of others.

If I depress my egotism, I express tolerance and a spirit of fraternity; if I express my desire to say a biting word even of one who has injured me, I depress envy and bigotry. When love comes up, hate goes down; when jealousy goes down, charity comes up.

We human beings are not wise enough or innocent enough to judge one another. And the only decision we can rightly make about our brother who is doing wrong is to admit it and to say: "We will leave him to God."

$\mathcal{I}$t is my business to beg for the poor of the world, and I know how much thought is given to the hungry, the lame, the blind, and the maimed. It is not that great feasts are to be condemned, but rather that the poor are to be remembered.

It is not possible to invite the poor of Asia and Africa and Oceania to our tables, but at least we can give to them a proportion of what we spend on the rich. King St. Louis IX of France did this very thing: He had two hundred poor persons dine with him every evening, and he personally served them at table.

Charity is a habit, not a gush or sentiment; it is a virtue, not an ephemeral thing of moods and impulses; it is a quality of the soul, rather than an isolated good deed.

So long as there are poor,
   I am poor;
So long as there are prisons,
   I am a prisoner;
So long as there are sick,
   I am weak;
So long as there is ignorance,
   I must learn the truth;
So long as there is hate,
   I must love;
So long as there is hunger,
   I am famished.

Such is the identification Our Divine Lord would have us make with all whom He made in love and for love.

A kind word gives encouragement to the despondent heart, and a cruel word makes others sob their way to the grave.

*H*elp someone in distress, and you lighten your own burden. The very joy of alleviating the sorrow of another is the lessening of one's own. If we dig someone else out of a hole, we get out of the hole we are in.

The real test of the Christian is not how much he loves his friends, but how much he loves his enemies.

Part Four

⬦

LIVING IN TRUTH

"How happy is he
born and taught
That serveth
not another's will;
Whose armour is
his honest thought,
And simple truth
his utmost skill."
—*Sir John Wotton,*
The Character of a Happy Life

$\mathcal{E}$very earthly ideal is lost by being possessed. The more material your ideal, the greater the disappointment; the more spiritual it is, the less the disillusionment.

$\mathcal{T}$here is nothing that so much adds to the longevity of sickness as a long face.

$\mathcal{G}$reat men tell the truth and are seldom believed. Lesser men are generally believed, though they seldom speak the truth.

People say that when they know, they will do; Christ says when we do, then we will know. The seeds of truth sprout in the soil of obedience.

If my ego is the determinant of right and wrong, then who can say I am anything but the good person I believe myself to be?

It is a mark of sanity to "talk to yourself," provided the subject is the real self.

One often hears speakers at banquets when they are given some cup, or diploma, or degree, or praise, answer: "I am very humble, but proud"—without ever thinking of how they could be both at the same time. Humility is like underwear: We have to have it, but we should never show it. Pride is what we think ourselves to be; humility is the truth we know about ourselves, not in the eyes of our neighbor, but in the eyes of God.

Silence for at least a quarter of an hour a day helps the distraught soul to do something besides "think"—namely, to be thoughtful.

In a very busy life the secret of getting things done is not so much to know what to do, but rather to know what to leave undone.

If everyone finally caught up with the Joneses, what a yearning there would be to be a non-Jones, a Smith, or an anti-Jones. Life would be a nightmare without differences, as would a harp with just one string.

No analysis of the water that goes into a sinking ship will save it; neither will the diagnosis of our national ills heal our wounds. In a more positive way, may I beg my fellow citizens to be less concerned with politics and be more concerned with ethics.

Time is too short in which to do everything; time is too long in which to leave good things unfinished. Meditation on the duties of the day not only eliminates trivia, it also intensifies resoluteness in what is basically one's vocation in life.

The one thing in the world that never changes is change. Unless there is something that does not change, we would never know we were changing.

In our present life, we are always involved in the future; the eternal is tied up with the temporal, the ideal is in tension with the fact; what we ought to be is connected with what we are; the "not yet" determines the "now," just as the medical student at every moment of his studies has before him the ideal of becoming an M.D.

*F*reedom which ignores the transcendent difference between good and evil ends in the denial of freedom itself.

*T*he so-called generation gap does not exist; it is a spirit-gap—the distance between the leaders who are not on fire with ideals and the followers who are unlighted torches waiting for the flame. The young are as quick to pick out phonies as they are anxious to be inspired by those who are unafraid of being unpopular once truth is at stake.

A person who has no contact with real, precious stones has no criteria by which to judge synthetic stones. If everyone sets his own watch to suit his "situation," will there ever be a correct time?

*H*umans live by their desires, but it is possible for us to choose whether we will desire things of the spirit or of the world. The person who can look back on his day and count five times when he has refused to yield to some minute whim is on the way to inner growth: He has held himself back and rejected the slavery of things.

There is never any self-expression without self-repression. If I repress the thought of stealing from a bank, I express honesty; if I repress a lie, I express myself in favor of truth; if I repress greed, I express my love of neighbor. Self-denial is not always easy. Rimbaud put it well: "Spiritual warfare is just as brutal as human warfare."

The only way to know how difficult it is to repress temptation is to ask someone who has.

$\mathcal{T}$rue compassion is made up of three inseparable elements: the fall from a standard; assured responsibility and repentance for the condition; rehabilitation through sacrifice.

$\mathcal{A}$ man preparing to go out for the evening to give a speech said to his wife: "How many wise men do you think there are in this country?" She answered: "One less than you think."

Those who elevate their own superiority imagine that others do not really appreciate their true worth.

A character is built by what we stand for; our reputation, which is quite different, by what we fall for.

A reason is something we give before a conclusion is reached; an excuse is something we give for not following out the conclusion. Reasons generally are sincere; excuses generally are a rationalization of conduct.

*T*o judge others keeps us at the circumference of life—and away from the center.

Over and above both information and knowledge is wisdom which is born of a virtuous life and the illumination of the spirit. It does not necessarily depend on learning, study, or education. Sometimes the uneducated possess wisdom to an eminent degree. The more saintly a person is the wiser he is, though he may have less education and less information. When comes a great crisis in life, when sorrow overwhelms, when one is tempted to take the shortcut to get ahead, always consult the virtuous and the wise.

The person who is too worldly has no standard of judgment outside the world himself; therefore, he can never be a judge of values. Only the one who thinks and lives in two spheres, the worldly and the spiritual, can truly counsel about either.

$\mathcal{E}$vil thoughts are best destroyed by good thoughts that crowd them, evil loves by stronger loves of the good. Saint Paul says, "Be not overcome by evil, but overcome evil by good." Evil is not to be fought, head-on, by mere brute willpower; it is better for us to flank it, to drive it from the field by a greater intensity of goodness, a greater love or God. A mind filled with ideas of love and beauty has little room for evil notions.

*E*very ship that makes a voyage, after fogs and storms have blackened the sky, seizes the first opportunity of a clearing light to make observations of its movements. So it is with ourselves. Even in our journey from earth to heaven we need harbors where we can relax and enter into ourselves.

Many of our activities have localized areas in the brain; when these are given over too much to the same activity, the same effect is produced as if the same muscles were strained in constant exertion. Even the idea that our entire life must be dedicated to the welfare of others, forgets that we do most for our fellowman when we do most for spiritualizing our soul.

The nearer the soul is to God, the less its disturbances, since the point nearest the circle is subject to the least motion.

The touchstone of our age is not value as it used to be, but pain. The whole effort of people is to push away pain, establish a distance to it, place oneself outside of its zone. The pleasure principle alone matters, and anything that delays pleasure is to be condemned.

*S*ociety will be saved by those who are not absorbed by news on the hour, but by those who have eternity in their heart and time on their hands.

*O*ne of the reasons why our culture is decaying is because our conduct is based on the fact that "everybody's doing it." Also, our "leaders" are not leaders, but followers of "everybody."

Moses is the type of leader we need. He was not conservative; he was not a leader. He was above both. He started a new people with the battle cry: "Who is with the Lord!"

Silence is a home-coming and a return to center. It is not simply an absence of words, for that can be awkward. Silence enables one to discover sacred meaning behind secular events, to examine one's goals, and to re-create the original unity of the world.

When we try to make everything clear, we make everything confused. If, however, we admit one mysterious thing in the universe, then everything else becomes clear in the light of that.

The key to a joyful life is: "What does it profit a man if he gain the whole world and lose his soul?" Nothing matters but the ability to take the hard things of the life, the defeat, the nasty word, the barbed shaft, and yet never let them sour or fester the spirit. There are saints in heaven who have been sinners, but no saint is ever admitted to heaven who is sad. The greatest walk in the freshness of morning, shouting Joy.

The quest for success may make us work so hard that we beget failure.

Too much emphasis is laid upon the fact that we must adjust ourselves to our environment and adjust ourselves to society. Rather, we must be self-adjusted by subordination of body to soul, senses to reason, reason to faith.

It is all very well to say that a good man should never have the flu and a good girl never have rain on the day of her wedding, but this is not the message of religion. God is not a Robin Hood who steals from gangsters to stuff the pockets of poor widows. He is no Harun-al-Rashid or legendary caliph of Baghdad who goes out at evening from his celestial palace to right all wrongs and reward virtuous ladies by a successful appearance on "Strike It Rich."

God often flies in the face of common sense in order to make sense.

*I*t could very well be that the quest for identity could be the quest for the selfish ego. Simone Weil wrote: "It is not my business to think about myself. My business is to think about God. It is for God to think about me." That is when listening begins.

$\mathcal{A}$ religion that mar-
ries the spirit of
the age always becomes a widow in the
nest. Perhaps many are giving up religion today because they cannot see
any difference between it and the
world. Once men ran from the sight
of the cross; now it hangs from necks,
often upside down, tortured like a
Nazi cross and locked in a circle and
made a symbol of false peace.

Once religion was not tried because it
was too hard; now it is not tried because it is too easy.

$\mathcal{G}$lumness produces what might be called "reduplication." The self is confronted with self. The story is told of a prisoner who escaped one night from a prison, walked all night, swam a river twice, and at sunrise found himself back at the very prison from which he escaped.

The glum person is like this: He is always trying to "get away from himself," but all the roads he takes are circular, and he meets himself coming back.

$\mathcal{W}$hen a nation has enough quiet souls to act as a leaven, the masses will rise from a dead conformity.

*I*t is very hard today for strong hands to remain clean. It is far easier for clean hearts to keep hands both clean and strong.

*P*ublic opinion is like a police officer; it helps to keep order in human life, but the heart knows when it is wrong, even in the midst of the applause of the world. The danger for most people lies not in the defiance of public repute, but in subservience to it and the acceptance of it as the final court of appeal. It has been said of Francis Bacon: "There was a deep and fatal flaw in him—he was a pleaser of men."

*C*ivilizations can break down. Because our own has defined freedom as the right to do whatever I please, instead of the right to do whatever I ought, we are on the precipice of a Moral Shock. Because our emphasis is placed on technology and the Gross National Product, what is happening to the soul of a nation is forgotten. Our pride in leading the world industrially can be a form of pride that only blinds us to the schism of soul.

As the ancient Chinese philosopher warns:

> He who stands on tip-toe
>   does not stand firm.
> He who takes the longest strides,
>   does not walk the fastest.

He who does his own looking
   sees little.
He who defines himself
   is not therefore distinct.
He who boasts of what he will
   do succeeds in nothing.
He who is proud of his work,
   achieves nothing that endures.

*I*s it any wonder that the young refuse to be churchgoing, if they can find nothing in it that they have not already adjusted to in the world?

While we develop every form of electronic device to protect outer defenses, why are we not concerned with the moral and spiritual disintegration in our homes and on our streets? As Yeats put it:

> Things fall apart;
>   the center cannot hold;
> Mere anarchy is loosed
>   upon the world,
> The blood-dimmed tide
>   is loosed, and everywhere
> The ceremony of innocence
>   is drowned.

There are no plains in the spiritual life. We are either going uphill or coming down.

If a person is forced to live in one room, he considers himself a captive. If he lives in a building with a thousand rooms, he seems to be freer, but he is not. Multiple choices of means are never a substitute for an end. Is the writer who has a choice of a thousand pencils more free to write a novel than he who has one?

To be on the move to new options never makes happiness.

Without a sense of creatureliness or dependence, there can be no worship. We have a duty to worship God, not because He will be unhappy if we do not, but because if we do not worship Him, we will be imperfect and unhappy.

In order to understand goodness, we must make a distinction between getting what we want and getting what we need. Is God good when He fulfills our wishes, or when we fulfill His? Is God good only when He gives us what we want, or is He good when He gives us what we need even though we do not want it?

The son of Confucius once said to his father: "I apply myself with diligence to every kind of study, neglect nothing that could render me clever and brilliant; but I do not advance." "Omit some of your pursuits and you will get on better," replied Confucius. "Among those who travel on foot, have you ever seen any who run? It is essential to do everything in order, and to grasp that which is within the reach of your arm; otherwise, you give yourself useless trouble. Those who, like yourself, desire to do everything in one day, do nothing to the end of their lives, while others who steadily adhere to one pursuit find that they have accomplished their purpose."

There is no quarreling with the fact that freedom does mean choice, but freedom does not mean an infinite number of choices. One eventually has to come to a final question: "What then?"

When Huxley wrote in 1932 his Brave New World, he described the New World as one in which there would be thousands of alternatives or options, like ships to take, but never a harbor. Life is like an airplane schedule—a variety of lines, a miscellany of departures, but no airports.

*P*eace is impossible without justice. To ask for peace without justice is to identify peace with tranquillity or absence of conflict. Robbers sitting about a table are tranquil in the possession of their spoils and in their escape from police, but justice is wanting. The best definition of peace is that of Augustine: "tranquillity with justice."

*F*reedom, if we only knew it, is within the law of our nature, not outside it. Try to be so progressive and broad-minded as to draw a giraffe with a short neck or a triangle with four sides, and see where you end.

It is easy to be identified with the mass-mind, for even dead bodies float downstream. The person who redirects a culture is one who stops the "rat race" in order to listen to a voice calling. What he wants to do with God's help is to create, as it were, a new species, a different race of men.

As an artist must stand away from his painting to really see it, so the leader stands apart from the mass-mind to give it a new spirit.

Treasures lie hidden in darkness. Only those who walk in the night ever see the stars.

Though the past is, to some extent, like a funeral gone by, complete neglect of it is dangerous to any age; ignoring it is like amnesia to the memory. Without it, we are apt to think that we have original ideas.

Humility is very beautiful when it is natural, but when cultivated like rouge on a cheek, it becomes distasteful.

In all the areas of life, the crowning charm of excellence is the unconsciousness of excellence. Self-oblivion of beauty, power, and learning is emancipation of the spirit and blessing.

Many times in Scripture we see the words "Fear not." The shepherds were warned by the angels to fear not; Our Lord told His frightened apostles to fear not; and after His Resurrection He prefaced His words on peace with "Fear not."

Our Lord warns us not to fear because there are three false fears that keep us from God: We want to be saved, but not from our sins; we want to be saved, but not at too great a cost; we want to be saved in our way, not His.

*I*t has often been said that a country gets the politicians it deserves. Perhaps, therefore, it is a mistake to expect our leaders to have more moral fiber than we have, at any given time. In that case, our duty as voters begins before we even go to the polls. Our first duty is clearly to strengthen ourselves, and to make ourselves worthy of better politicians. If there is dishonesty and selfishness in our own souls, we can hardly expect to find anything better in the souls of men who represent us. Only when our own moral standards are better can we look for better legislation.

To find the Infinity we crave, we must also have the help of infinity. God is not only our goal. He is also the way by which we get there, and the life we need on our journey. He is the source of spiritual energy, bringing us the strength and wisdom to realize our cravings and to transcend our natures.

Other forms of energy may carry us to the furthest stars. But only Divine energy can get us to rise above ourselves.

When one gets down to the bottom of the subject of freedom, it becomes clear that we are less free than free-able. We may increase or decrease our inner freedom as we live. The more one is dominated by externals, the less he is in control of himself and, therefore, free.

A child is cute so long as he does not know that he is cute. As soon as he thinks he is, he turns into a brat. True beauty is unconscious; conscious beauty often becomes arrogant.

*D*ryness in the spiritual life and in marriage are actually graces. God's finger is stirring the waters of the soul, creating discontent, that efforts may be put forth.

There are two kinds of dryness: one that rots, and this is the dryness of love without God; the other is the dryness that ripens, and that is won when one grows through the fires and heat of sacrifice.

$\mathcal{M}$ost people assume that there is only one way to prevent wars, and that is by a horizontal action of one group or another group, in the manner of two billiard balls, one force resisting another. But, actually, besides horizontal there is a vertical action. Vertical action implies one part of the world contacting God, in order that He might influence another part of the world who resists Him. Instead of human-human contact as in war, there is the human-divine-human contact in prayer. As the heat of the sun's ray is intensified by passing through a magnifying glass, so the power of man is magnified by passing through Divinity!

*T*he higher the build-
ing, the deeper the
foundation; the greater the aspiration,
the more rarefied the humility.

*T*he Christmas mes-
sage is not that
peace will come automatically, because
Christ is born in Bethlehem; that birth
in Bethlehem was the prelude to His
birth in our hearts by grace and faith
and love. Peace belongs only to those who
will to have it. If there is no peace in
the world today, it is not because
Christ did not come; it is because we
did not let Him in.

*T*he humble person knows that there are two things said about him that are untrue: things that are too good to be true; and things that are too bad to be true.

*G*od sets many angels in our paths, but often we know them not; in fact, we may go through life never knowing that they were agents or messengers of God to lead us on to virtue or to deter us from vice. But they symbolize that constant and benign intervention of God in the history of men, which stops us on the path of destruction or leads us to success or happiness and virtue.

Welcomed or re-
jected, recog-
nized or ignored, God is in every fold
of our nature.

We always make
the mistake of
thinking that it is what we do that
matters, when really what matters is
what we let God do to us. God sent
the angel to Mary, not to ask her to
do something, but to let something be
done.

We do not pray in order that we may change God's will; rather, we pray to change our own.

In each child, God whispers a new secret to the world; adds a new dimension of immortality to creation.

The more ties we have to earth, the harder will it be for us to die.

$\mathcal{T}$he consolation Our Lord gives is not always to cool our fevered brow or heal our broken limb, but to give us a vision of His purposes.

$\mathcal{T}$here is not a critical person in the world who is not in need of criticism.

$\mathcal{E}$very expenditure of human strength that makes what is a means an end, which isolates living from the goal of living, is a busy idleness, a sad and mournful reality.

This is the choice before us: Either try to revolutionize the world and break under it, or revolutionize ourselves and remake the world.

Most people demand of their neighbor much more than God demands of him.

Souls are sometimes closest to God when they feel themselves farthest away from Him, at the point of despair.

$\mathcal{E}$very moment comes to you pregnant with a Divine Purpose; time being so precious that God deals it out only second by second. Once it leaves your hands and your power to do with it as you please, it plunges into eternity— to remain forever whatever you made it.

ABOUT THE AUTHOR

Archbishop Fulton J. Sheen (1895–1979), one of the most notable Catholic prelates of all time, was a gifted orator, writer, preacher, and educator. He earned a J.C.B. from Catholic University in Washington, D.C. (where he later taught philosophy), a Ph.D. from Louvain University in Belgium, an S.T.D. from the Angelicum in Rome, and other degrees, including numerous honorary degrees.

The author of scores of books in the areas of theology, philosophy, Christian living, and spirituality, Sheen is also fondly remembered as a master of the media. In addition to his radio broadcast, "Catholic Hour," and the award-winning television series, "Life Is Worth Living," he wrote regular weekly newspaper columns—syndicated in both the religious and secular press—for more than two decades.